Tim Rice
& Andrew Lloyd Webber

JOSEPH
and the Amazing Technicolor® Dreamcoat

with pictures by
Quentin Blake

PAVILION
MICHAEL JOSEPH

First published in 1982 by
Pavilion Books Limited
196 Shaftesbury Avenue, London WC2H 8JL
in association with Michael Joseph Limited
44 Bedford Square London WC1B 3DU

Words in this form by Tim Rice
The libretto of the musical work JOSEPH AND THE AMAZING
TECHNICOLOR DREAMCOAT is reproduced by permission of
Novello & Company Limited
'Technicolor' is the registered trademark of Technicolor, Inc.
Copyright © Novello & Company Limited 1982
Illustrations Copyright © Quentin Blake 1982

Printed in Italy   ISBN 0-907516-02-5

Rice, Tim
    Joseph and the amazing technicolor
dreamcoat.
1. Musical revues, comedies, etc.,
Juvenile — librettos
I. Title II. Lloyd Webber, Andrew
III. Blake, Quentin
782.81'2   ML50.R/

FOREWORD by Tim Rice

Something new seems to happen nearly every year to the fifteen-minute entertainment that Andrew Lloyd Webber and I wrote for Alan Doggett, the music master at Colet Court School, in 1968. From that humble beginning, *Joseph* has been performed by schools, amateur drama groups and professional companies (including five separate runs in the West End) all over the world. It has been a television special, the music has been featured on numerous records, and discussions about a movie version have been pottering along for ages. Every schoolchild and ex-schoolchild I meet seems to have 'done *Joseph*' during their formative years. Although it makes me feel a little long in the tooth to be told by a father of three that he played Potiphar at the age of fourteen, I am always delighted to hear of the continuing success of *Joseph* in schools, because it was written for schoolchildren. Any other versions are really just a welcome bonus.

The work has grown in size along the way – by subtle use of reprises, encores and a lengthy interval at half-time, a crafty theatre director can now spin *Joseph* out to last a good two hours – but I hope that the original spirit of the piece has never been lost as a result of expansion. It's a spirit that Quentin Blake has captured perfectly in his illustrations for this book. I realize that without the music a vital element of the work is missing, but arrogantly I like to think that the words on their own are still capable of providing entertainment, and there is no question that Quentin's paintings do. Anyway, there is nothing to stop readers singing the words aloud if they are unable to appreciate the story without Andrew Lloyd Webber's melodies. Alternatively, look upon this book as a way of enjoying *Joseph* silently – something, I am glad to say, that few theatre audiences have done so far.

January 1982

Way way back many centuries ago, not long after the Bible
 began
Jacob lived in the land of Canaan, a fine example of a family
 man
Jacob, Jacob and Sons, depended on farming to earn their
 keep
Jacob, Jacob and Sons, spent all of the days in the fields
 with sheep
Jacob was the founder of a whole new nation, thanks to the
 number of children he'd had
He was also known as Israel but most of the time his sons
 and his wives used to call him dad
Jacob, Jacob and Sons – men of the soil, of the sheaf and
 crook
Jacob, Jacob and Sons – a remarkable family in anyone's
 book
Reuben was the eldest of the children of Israel, with
 Simeon and Levi the next in line
Napthali and Isaachar with Asher and Dan, Zebulun and
 Gad took the total to nine
Jacob, Jacob and Sons – Benjamin and Judah, which leaves
 only one:
Joseph – Jacob's favourite son

Joseph's mother – she was Jacob's favourite wife
He never really loved another all his life
And Joseph was his joy because
He reminded him of her
Through young Joseph Jacob lived his life again
Loved him, praised him, gave him all he could – but then
It made the rest feel second best
And even if they were . . .
Being told 'you're also-rans'
Did not make them Joseph fans

And where we have really missed the boat is
We're great guys but no-one seems to notice

Joseph's charm and winning smiles
Failed to slay them in the aisles
And their father couldn't see the danger
He could not imagine any danger
He just saw in Joseph all his dreams come true
Jacob wanted to show the world he loved his son
To make it clear that Joseph was the special one
So Jacob bought his son a coat
A multi-coloured coat to wear
Joseph's coat was elegant, the cut was fine
The tasteful style was the ultimate in good design
And this is why
It caught the eye
A king would stop and stare

And when Joseph tried it on
He knew his sheepskin days were gone
Such a dazzling coat of many colours
How he loved his coat of many colours
In a class above the rest
It even went well with his vest
Such a stunning coat of many colours
How he loved his coat of many colours
It was red and yellow and green and brown and blue

Joseph's brothers weren't too pleased with what they saw
They had never liked him all that much before

And now this coat
Had got their goat
They felt life was unfair
And when Joseph graced the scene
His brothers turned a shade of green
His astounding clothing took the biscuit
Quite the smoothest person in the district
He looked handsome, he looked smart, he was a walking
    work of art
Such a dazzling coat of many colours
It was red and yellow and green and brown
And scarlet and black and ochre and peach
And ruby and olive and violet and fawn
And lilac and gold and chocolate and mauve
And azure and lemon and russet and grey
And purple and white and pink and orange and blue!

Joseph's coat annoyed his brothers
But what really made them mad
Were the things that Joseph told them of the dreams he'd
    often had

Joseph's First Dream
I dreamed that in the fields one day at corn-collecting time
Your eleven sheaves of corn all turned and bowed to mine
My sheaf was quite a sight to see, a golden sheaf and tall
Yours were green and second-rate and really rather small

This was not the kind of thing the brothers liked to hear
It seemed to them that Joseph and his dreams should
    disappear

Joseph's Second Dream

I dreamed I saw eleven stars, the sun and moon and sky
bowing down before my star – it made me wonder why
Could it be that I was born for higher things than you?
A post in someone's government, a ministry or two?

Brothers

These dreams of our dear brother are the decade's biggest yawn
His talk of stars and golden sheaves is just a load of corn
Not only is he tactless but he's also rather dim
For there's eleven of us and there's only one of him
The dreams of course will not come true
That is we think they won't come true
That is we hope they won't come true –
What if he's right all along?

The dreams were more than crystal clear, the writing on the
    wall
Meant that Joseph some day soon would rise above them all
The accuracy of the dreams the brothers did not know
But one thing they were sure about – the dreamer had to go

Next day, far from home, the brothers planned the
    repulsive crime

Let us grab him now, do him in while we've got the time

This they did and made the most of it
Tore his coat and flung him in a pit

Let us leave him here – all alone – he's bound to die

Then some Ishmaelites, a hairy crew, came riding by
In a flash the brothers changed their plan

We need cash! Let's sell him if we can
Could you use a slave, you hairy bunch of Ishmaelites?
Young, strong, well-behaved, going cheap and he reads and
        writes

In a trice the dirty deal was done
Silver coins for Jacob's favourite son
So the Ishmaelites galloped off with a slave in tow
Off to Egypt where Joseph was not keen to go
It wouldn't be a picnic he could tell
And he didn't speak Egyptian very well
Joseph's brothers tore his precious multi-coloured coat
Having ripped it up they next attacked a passing goat
Soon the wretched creature was no more
They dipped the coat in blood and guts and gore
Oh those brothers, how low could they stoop?
They made a sordid group, hey, how low could they stoop?
Poor poor Joseph, sold to be a slave
Situation's grave, hey, sold to be a slave

Brothers
Father we've something to tell you
A story of our time
A tragic but inspiring tale
Of manhood in its prime
You know you had a dozen sons – well now that's not quite true
But feel no sorrow, do not grieve – he would not want you to
Joseph died as he wished to
He answered duty's call
He single-handed fought the beast
That would have killed us all
His blood-stained coat is tribute to his final sacrifice
His body may be past its peak but his soul's in Paradise
When we think of his last great battle
A lump comes to the throat
It takes a man who knows not fear
To wrestle with a lion – er, goat
Carve his name with pride and courage
Let no tear be shed
If he had not laid down his life
We all would now be dead

There's one more angel in heaven
There's one more star in the sky
Joseph we'll never forget you
It's tough but we're gonna to get by
There's one less place at our table
There's one more tear in our eye
But Joseph the things that you stood for
Like love and peace – like truth and light – like democracy –
    never die

Joseph was taken to Egypt in chains and sold
Where he was bought by a captain named Potiphar . . .
Potiphar had very few cares
He was one of Egypt's millionaires
Having made a fortune buying shares in pyramids
Potiphar had made a huge pile
Owned a large percentage of the Nile
Meant that he could really live in style and he did

Joseph was an unimportant slave who found he liked his
    master
Consequently worked much harder, even with devotion
Potiphar could see that Joseph was a cut above the average
Made him leader of his household – maximum promotion

Potiphar was cool and so fine
But his wife would never toe the line
It's all there in chapter thirty-nine of Genesis
She was beautiful but evil
Saw a lot of men against his will
Potiphar however thought she still was his
Joseph's looks and handsome figure had attracted her
    attention
Every morning she would beckon:
'Come and lie with me, love'
Joseph wanted to resist her till one day she proved too
    eager
Joseph cried in vain 'Please stop, I don't believe in free love'

Potiphar was counting shekels in his den below the bed-
    room
When he heard a mighty rumpus clattering above him
Suddenly he knew his riches couldn't buy him what he
    wanted
Gold could never make him happy if she didn't love him
Letting out a mighty roar
Potiphar burst through the door

Joseph I'll see you rot in jail
The things you have done are beyond the pale!

Poor poor Joseph locked up in a cell
Things aren't going well, hey, locked up in a cell

Close every door to me, hide all the world from me
Bar all my windows and shut out the light
Do what you want with me, hate me and laugh at me
Darken my daytime and torture my night
Just give me a number instead of my name
Forget all about me and let me decay
I do not matter, I'm only one person
Destroy me completely, then throw me away
If my life were important I would ask will I live or die
But I know the answers lie far from this world
Close every door to me, keep those I love from me
Children of Israel are never alone
For we know we shall find our own peace of mind
For we have been promised a land of our own

Joseph's luck was really out, his spirit and his fortune low
Alone he sat, alone he thought of happy times he used to
　　know
The prison walls were wet and black, his chains were heavy
　　and weighed him down
A candle was his only light, the hungry rats the only sound

Then one day the door was opened, in were flung two
frightened men
Neither thought that they would ever see the light of day
again
Both men were servants of Pharaoh the king
Both in the doghouse for doing their thing
One was a baker, a cook in his prime
One was a butler, the Jeeves of his time

Hey Joseph help us if you can
We've had dreams that we don't understand

Joseph
Tell me your dreams my friends and I will tell you what they
show
Though I cannot guarantee to get it right I'll have a go

First the butler, trembling, took the floor
Nervously he spoke of what he saw

There I was standing in front of a vine
I picked me some grapes and I crushed them to wine
I gave them to Pharaoh who drank from my cup
I tried to interpret but I had to give up

Joseph
You will soon be free old chap so do not worry any more
The king will let you out of here, you'll buttle as you did before

Next the baker rose to tell his dream
Hoping it would have a similar theme

There I was standing with baskets of bread
High in the sky I saw birds overhead
Who flew to the baskets and ate every slice
Give me the message, I need your advice

Joseph
Sad to say your dream is not the kind of dream I'd like to get
Pharaoh has it in for you, your execution date is set
Don't rely on all I said I saw
It's just that I have not been wrong before

Go go go Joseph you know what they say
Sha la la Joseph you'll make it one day
Hang on now Joseph you're doing fine
You and your dreamcoat, ahead of your time

Pharaoh he was a powerful man
With the ancient world in the palm of his hand
To all intents and purposes he
Was Egypt with a capital E
Whatever he did he was showered with praise
If he cracked a joke then you chortled for days
No-one had rights or a vote but the king
In fact you might say he was fairly right-wing
When Pharaoh's around then you get down on the ground
If you ever find yourself near Rameses
Get down on your knees

But down at the other end of the scale
Joseph was still doing time in jail
For even though he was in with the guards
A lifetime in prison was still on the cards
But though Joseph's prospects were not looking bright
At the end of the tunnel was a glimmer of light
For all of a sudden there were visions and things
Disturbing the sleep of both peasants and kings
Strange as it seems there'd been a run of crazy dreams
And a man who could interpret would go far
Could become a star
Could be famous, could be a big success

Guess what? In his bed Pharaoh had an uneasy night
He had had a dream that pinned him to his sheets with
    fright
No-one knew the meaning of the dream
What to do? Whatever could it mean?
Then some lively lad said
He knew of a bloke in jail
Who was hot on dreams, could explain old Pharaoh's tale
Pharaoh said –

Fetch this Joseph man
I need him to help me if he can

Chained and bound, afraid, alone
Joseph stood before the throne

My service to Pharaoh has begun
Tell me your problems, mighty one

*I was wandering along the banks of the river when seven fat
    cows came up out of the Nile
And right behind these fine healthy animals came seven other
    cows that were skinny and vile
And then the thin cows ate the fat cows which I thought would
    do them good
But no it didn't make them fatter like such a monster supper
    should
The thin cows were as thin as they had ever ever been
This dream has got me baffled, hey Joseph what does it mean?
Now you know that kings ain't stupid
But I don't have a clue
So don't be cruel Joseph
Help me now I beg of you . . .*

*Then I was standing doing nothing in a field out of town when I
    saw seven beautiful ears of corn
They were ripe, they were golden, but you've guessed it – right
    behind them there were seven other ears that were tattered
    and torn
Then the bad corn ate the good corn, they came up from behind,
    yes they did
But Joseph here's the punchline I think it's going to blow your
    mind, flip your lid
The bad corn was as bad as it had ever ever been
This dream has got me all shook up, treat me nice and tell me
    what it means
Hey, hey Joseph won't you tell poor old Pharaoh
What does it mean?*

Seven years of bumper crops are on their way
Years of plenty, endless wheat and tons of hay
Your farms will boom, there won't be room
To store the surplus food you grow

After that the future doesn't look so bright
Egypt's luck will change completely overnight
And famine's hand will stalk the land
With food an all-time low

Noble king there is no doubt
What your dream is all about
All these things you saw in your pyjamas
Are a long-range forecast for your farmers
And I'm sure it's crossed your mind
What it is you have to find
Find a man to lead you through the famine
With a flair for economic planning
But who this man would be I just don't know

Pharaoh

Well stone the crows this Joseph is a clever kid
Who'd have thought that fourteen cows could mean the things
    he says they did?

Joseph, you must help me further, I have got a job for you
You shall lead us through this crisis, you shall be my number
    two

Pharaoh told his guards to fetch a chisel from the local store
Whereupon he ordered them to cut the chains that Joseph
    wore
Joseph got a royal pardon and a host of splendid things
A chariot of gold, a cloak, a medal and some signet rings
Seven summers on the trot were perfect just as Joseph said
Joseph saw that food was gathered ready for the years
    ahead
Seven years of famine followed, Egypt did not mind a bit
The first recorded rationing in history was a hit

Adoring Girls

Joseph how can we ever say
All we want to about you
We're so glad you came our way
We would have perished without you

Pharaoh
Joseph we are the perfect team
Old buddies that's you and me
I was wise to have chosen you
You will be wise to agree
We were in a jam – would have baffled Abraham
But now we're a partnership it's just a piece of cake

Girls
Greatest man since Noah
Only goes to shoah

Joseph
Anyone from anywhere can make it, if they get a lucky break

This could be a happy ending, perfect place to stop the
    show
Joseph after all has got about as far as he could go
But I'm sure that Jacob and his other sons have crossed your
    mind
How had famine hit the family Joseph left behind?

Do you remember the good years in Canaan?
The summers were endlessly gold
The fields were a patchwork of clover
The winters were never too cold
We strolled down the boulevards together
And everything round us was fine
Now the fields are dead and bare
No joie de vivre anywhere
Et maintenant we drink a bitter wine

Those Canaan days we used to know
Where have they gone? Where did they go?
Eh bien, raise your berets to those Canaan days
Do you remember those wonderful parties?
The splendours of Canaan's cuisine
Our extravagant elegant soirées
The gayest the Bible has ever seen
It's funny but since we lost Joseph
We've gone to the other extreme
No-one comes to dinner now
We'd only eat them anyhow
We even find we're missing Joseph's dreams

It's funny but since we lost Joseph
We've gone to the other extreme
Perhaps we all misjudged the lad
Perhaps he wasn't quite that bad
And how we miss his entertaining dreams

Yes back in Canaan the future looked rough
Jacob's family were finding it tough
For the famine had caught them unprepared
They were thin, they were ill, they were getting scared
It was enough to make anyone weep
They were down to their very last sheep

We will starve if we hang around here
And in Egypt there's food going spare
They got corn, they got meat, they got fruit and drinks
And if we have the time we could see the Sphinx

So they finally decided to go
Off to Egypt to see brother Jo
So they all lay before Joseph's feet
And begged him for something to eat
Joseph found it a strain not to laugh because
Not a brother among them knew who he was

Joseph
I shall now take them all for a ride
After all they have tried fratricide

(I dreamed that in the fields one day at corn-collecting time
Your eleven sheaves of corn all turned and bowed to mine
I dreamed I saw eleven stars, the sun the moon and sky
Bowing down before my star – it made me wonder why)

How do I know where you come from? You could be spies
Telling me that you are hungry – that could be lies
How do I know who you are?
Why do you think I should help you? Would you help me?
Why on earth should I believe you? I've no guarantee

Brothers
Grovel grovel cringe bow stoop fall
Worship worship beg kneel sponge crawl
We are just eleven brothers – good men and true
Though we know we count for nothing when up next to you
Honesty's our middle name
Life is slowly ebbing from us – hope's almost gone
It's getting very hard to see us from sideways on

Joseph
I rather like the way you're talking – astute and sincere
Suddenly your tragic story gets me right here
All this tugging at my heart strings seems quite justified
I shall give you all you came for – and a lot more beside

Joseph handed them sackloads of food
And they grovelled with base gratitude
Then unseen Joseph nipped out around the back
And planted a cup in young Benjamin's sack
When the brothers were ready to go
Joseph turned to them all with a terrible stare and said

No! No! No! No!
No! Stop you robbers, your little number's up
One of you has stolen my precious golden cup

Joseph started searching through his brothers' sacks
Everyone was nervous – no-one could relax
Who's the thief?

Is it Reuben? No!

Is it Simeon? No!

Is it Napthali? No!

Is it Dan? No!

Is it Asher? No!

Is it Isaachar? No!

Is it Levi? No!

Is it Zebulun? No!

Is it Gad? No!

Is it Judah? No!

Could it be – could it be –
Could it possibly be Benjamin?
Yes! Yes! Yes!

Benjamin you nasty youth, your crime has shocked me to the
*   core*
Never in my whole career have I encountered this before
Guards! Seize him! Lock him in a cell!
Throw the keys into the Nile as well!

Each of the brothers fell to his knees

Show him some mercy O mighty one please
He would not do this – he must have been framed
Jail us and beat us – we should be blamed
Oh no, not he
How you can accuse him is a mystery
Save him, take me
Benjamin is straighter than the tall palm tree
I hear the steel drums sing their song
They're singing man you know you got it wrong
I hear the voice of the yellow bird
Singing in the tree this is quite absurd
Oh yes it's true
Benjamin is straighter than the big bamboo
No ifs, no buts
Benjamin is honest as coconuts
Sure as the tide washes the golden sands
Benjamin is an innocent man
Sure as bananas need the sun
We are the guilty criminal ones
Oh no, not he
How you can accuse him is a mystery
Save him, take me
Benjamin is straighter than the tall palm tree

And Joseph knew by this his brothers now were honest
 men
The time had come at last to reunite them all again

Joseph
Can't you recognize my face? Is it hard to see
That Joseph who you thought was dead – your brother – is me?

Brothers
Joseph! Joseph! Is it really true?
Joseph! Joseph! Is it really you?

So Jacob came to Egypt
No longer feeling old
And Joseph went to meet him in his chariot of gold

I closed my eyes, drew back the curtain
To see for certain what I thought I knew
Far far away someone was weeping
But the world was sleeping, any dream will do
I wore my coat with golden lining
Bright colours shining, wonderful and new
And in the east the dawn was breaking
And the world was waking, any dream will do
A crash of drums, a flash of light
My golden cloak flew out of sight
The colours faded into darkness, I was left alone
May I return to the beginning
The light is dimming and the dream is too
The world and I, we are still waiting
Still hesitating, any dream will do
Give me my coloured coat, my amazing coloured coat

JOSEPH IN PERFORMANCE by Andrew Lloyd Webber

Joseph was premiered on the afternoon of 1 March 1968 to an audience of reluctant parents at St Paul's Junior School in London. It was the first work by Lloyd Webber and Rice to be publicly performed. It was composed for the school choir and lasted twenty-five minutes. *Joseph* was repeated in a concert at the Central Hall, Westminster, where it was favourably reviewed in the London *Sunday Times*. The work was then expanded and recorded.

Joseph was written to be performed by schools and colleges. Its American debut took place in May, 1970, at the College of the Immaculate Conception in Douglastown, Long Island. Since that time it has been widely performed by schools all over the world.

There have been various professional productions of *Joseph* which have normally achieved success in inverse proportion to their ambition. It was presented in 1972 by the Young Vic at the Edinburgh Festival in a production which was expanded and transferred to the West End of London in 1973. Since then, it has become an annual Christmas presentation in the West End.

In the United States it has been presented professionally, including two seasons at the Brooklyn Academy of Music and a long run in Washington, D.C. A televised version of *Joseph* was made in 1972. The recording, produced by Tim and myself on MCA records in 1972, contains most of the material in this new version. The first Broadway production transferred from the Entermedia Theatre, following a successful off-Broadway run, to the Royale Theatre and opened on the 27 January 1982.